Your Guide to Self-Publishing

Head Office:
New Generation Publishing, 107-111 Fleet Street,
London, EC4A 2AB

Buckinghamshire Office:
New Generation Publishing, Olney House, 17 High Street, Olney,
Buckinghamshire, MK46 4EB

01234 711 956
0207 936 9941
info@newgeneration-publishing.com

www.newgeneration-publishing.com
@NGPublishing

Contents

Current Publishing Industry

Over the last fifteen years the book industry has changed more rapidly than at any point in over a century. Much of this change has been caused by the rise of the Internet.

Fifteen years ago, traditional publishers published a certain type of book to be published in a certain outlet and publishers and high-street retailers held full control of the industry.

First to disrupt this were the online retailers, such as Amazon, who could list millions of books as available and, with low overheads and large resources, could price lower than the high-street bookshops. Then came the supermarkets, seeing an opportunity in the popularity of books to sell them at a loss in order to get strong footfall into their large stores.

And then there have been the changes in technology: the rise of print-on-demand, whereby books can be printed one at a time rather than in large and high-priced print runs; and the ebook, in tune with a market where digital demand is soaring.

As a result, traditional publishers have faced challenges with fewer outlets to sell stock into and at high discounts, leaving little room for profit. Most are currently facing the need to completely change their business model, and to look at the self-publishing model and print-on-demand services as an option for some of their backlist.

Self-Publishing has now become an industry-accepted route for authors to get their work published and into the market. With the ability to create their own books at a reasonable level of investment, in both print and digital formats, and to have them available globally, authors saw a viable alternate, making self-publishing more popular than it has ever been.

What is Self-Publishing?

Self-publishing offers authors an opportunity to become published without the need of having to go through a literary agent or a traditional publisher.

How does it work?
The following is the most common way in which self-publishing works:

An author will choose a publishing package that fits their needs, requirements and budget, and the author will have a member of staff who will answer any questions and advise them accordingly.

The author's manuscript is sent to the publisher as a word document, which the publisher will edit (if requested by the author), typeset to an agreed book size, and this document will then be sent back to the author as a PDF for approval.

At this stage, the author may notice some changes that they would like to make to the manuscript, and a form is supplied by the publisher asking the author to list the changes required. These changes are made and an amended PDF is sent to the author for approval.

The same process then happens for the cover design.

Once both the cover design and text have been signed off, the ISBN number is assigned to the book and the files are then sent to the printer. Once the book is approved at the printer, the bibliographic data is sent to the retailers and wholesalers, making the book available for sale throughout the world.

Now it is time for marketing and promotion.
The vast majority of self-publishing companies will sell additional marketing and promotional services. However, it is important that these services are explained in detail so that the author is buying the

correct service. The golden rule is: do not purchase services that you can do yourself.

It is also important that the author receives marketing and promotional support as and when they require, by phone or email, at no additional cost. A good self-publishing company will recognise that supporting the author in this way will increase their chances of selling more books and receiving more media coverage.

A good and respected self-publishing company will recognise that book sales are more important than sales of add-on services.

Why Self-Publish?

Self-Publishing is the quickest and most direct route to make your book available to a worldwide market.

With the majority of traditional publishers increasingly reluctant to take a risk on new authors, self-publishing has become a viable alternative.

Traditional publishers are looking for a guaranteed return when they publish a book, which is why the market is flooded with existing well-known authors and celebrities.

To look at it from their point-of-view, you can understand their strategy; they are a business that needs to make money. However, the situation leaves very little opportunity for a new author to find a literary agent or a traditional publisher.

With self-publishing, all that is required for you, the author, is to be writing or have written a book and a good self-publishing company should take care of the rest.

When looking for a self-publishing company to publish your book, ensure they can offer you the following:

- Personal support
- Global distribution
- Competitive retail pricing
- Tangible marketing services
- A real office
- The option to meet the publisher (if required)
- Experience

Always ask if you can meet, always ask what your published book will retail for, always ask for an example of the distribution and availability of their books. Many companies claim to offer this, but many can't actually provide it.

Self-Publishing offers authors complete flexibility and control over their book production and distribution. With advances in digital print it is possible to produce just a few copies at low cost without committing to large print runs.

Authors have many different reasons to self-publish. These could range from not being accepted by traditional publishing companies to desiring full control and artistic freedom.

A New Generation in Self-Publishing

New Generation Publishing is the UK's fastest growing self-publishing company with over 5,000 titles in print. With the rapid growth of options available to writers looking to get published, New Generation Publishing provides everything a writer would receive from self-publishers and traditional publishers, and more.

As the first self-publishing company to offer a bookseller service, and the first to provide access to digital sales, New Generation Publishing is the place for writers looking to get published.

We offer five book publishing packages to fully cover a writer's requirements from a publisher: Standard, Advanced, Premier, Bookseller and Bestseller. In addition, we offer a range of marketing services for writers, such as ebook conversion and distribution, press releases, advertising in *Writers' Forum* magazine, and more. Our editing services for authors range from proofreading through to a full critique and reader's report. Whatever your requirements are as an author, New Generation Publishing can help.

Publishing a book with NGP also offers you, the author, a personal service. Our team are on hand to offer you advice on publishing, editing, ebooks, marketing and promotion, and this advice is available before, during and, importantly, after publication.

Why New Generation Publishing?

- Full range of production as required, from typesetting and cover design to full editing.

- Full range of formats – from black and white to colour, paperback and hardback, print and ebook editions.

- Worldwide distribution and a wide range of marketing services, from press releases, media kits, to custom built websites and retail and magazine advertisements.

- Bookselling service: a dedicated bookseller to visit individual stores to sell your book on your behalf.

- UK-based company, with global distribution and print facilities, reaching over 40,000 retailers.

- Competitive retail pricing.

- A personal one-to-one service

Who Self-Publishes?

New Generation Publishing talks to all types of authors every day who are looking to publish their book.

Every author is different and every author's needs and requirements are different. New Generation Publishing is equipped to work with all authors who want to self-publish their book.

Let's take a look at the different types of authors:

Career authors
This is the author who wants to make a career out of writing and publishing. In most situations the goal of this writer is to be published traditionally and give up the day job to become a full-time author.

In some cases, the author has received rejection letters from agents and publishers and this is often nothing to do with the quality of their work – more often than not it is because their book does not fit with the agent or publisher. In many cases, it is because the publisher does not want to take on the risk of a new author, preferring instead to rely on their stable of existing authors and celebrities who will guarantee a return.

The option of self-publishing gives the author a chance to prove themselves in the market and create a business track record to show an agent or publisher that they are less of a risk.

Let's face it, if an agent or a publisher is approached by an author who has self-published a book, proved the book has a market (based on their sales and reviews), then it is likely they will be taken more seriously as a potential author for them to work with.

New Generation Publishing works with many of these authors and has the publishing options available to help you become a published author and reach your market.

Business authors

It has long been said that the 'book is the new business card' and many business owners are promoting themselves and their businesses by self-publishing a book. With the majority of business owners needing to promote their products and company as quickly as possible, the option of self-publishing their book and getting it on the market in two to three months can give them an edge on competitors.

The published book can also be used at talks, seminars and presentations, impressing existing and potential clients while also increasing credibility and revenue.

In addition, there are writers who make a business solely out of their book, highlighting a market, promoting to it and selling high numbers of copies with a positive financial return.

New Generation Publishing has the experience to offer and advise all types of business author.

Niche authors

Many authors realise that the subject matter of their book may not appeal to a wide market, and they understand that self-publishing is an appropriate route to guarantee that their book is published and made available to a global market. With the correct marketing, their niche audience can be easily reached, books can be sold, and reviews and revenue can be generated.

If you contact New Generation Publishing today we will be happy to advise you on your publishing options.

Legacy authors
Some authors simply want their book published! And why not?

You have written a book that has been in the top drawer of your desk for months, maybe years. Some people have read it and like it, so why not publish it and make it available to a global audience, and have it available for friends and family to buy now and in years to come? It might be a family history or a subject of local interest; whatever the genre or subject, New Generation Publishing can take your manuscript and turn it into a published book.

Whatever type of author you are, New Generation Publishing is happy to offer every author a free consultation to discuss their book, self-publishing and marketing, to help you decide on the best way forward.

Should You Publish Your Own Book?

If you have a book that doesn't fit inside the traditional publishing model, you may still have a book that turns a profit, communicates your message, and helps you to build your network.

Here's a short checklist to help you determine whether you should publish your own book:

- Do you know what purpose you want your book to serve?
- Do you know who your audience is? Finding a specific audience is a better sales tool than saying, "everyone will like my book."
- Have you researched the market to make sure other books of the same type are selling well (or ranking well in search engines and with book distributors)?
- Have you researched the market to make sure that your book is different than other books of the same type (in a good way)?
- Have you talked to other people about whether they would buy your book – not family and friends, but members of your audience?

If you have positive answers to these questions, you probably have a book worth taking through the self-publishing process.

Perfecting Your Work

Editing

You have worked tirelessly on your manuscript, you have received good feedback from friends, family, book groups, peer review sites, and so on, who think it is ready to be published.

You have signed up for a publishing package that will provide all the production, marketing, and sales services that you require to create a beautiful product and to make it available to the customers around the world.

However, the one difference often highlighted between traditional and self-publishing is editing – that layer of additional work that takes a manuscript from having potential to being great.

Some authors work with their own editor; some edit themselves and have the skills to perform both roles of author and editor. Though if you don't fit into either of these categories, your self-publishing company should be able to offer editing services, with the editing completed by professional, qualified editors.

Note the difference between editing and proofreading (see the next page). Editing is more structural, removing structural errors and line-by-line improving the work. New Generation Publishing will be happy to discuss its editing service with you – just ask!

Perfecting Your Work

Proofreading

Now that the rough diamond of your work has been polished up during editing, this isn't quite the end. You need to ensure all of those typos and small errors that inevitably creep in, but stick out painfully when published, are removed.

A lot of authors confuse editing and proofreading. Editors will often pick up the small errors, but when they are editing a work they are looking more at the overall picture.

Proofreading is the basic corrections – picking up and correcting spelling and grammar mistakes, repeated words, and other basic errors.

It is always a pity to come that far with your book, get a beautiful finished product but then find there are a number of errors that disappoint the reader.

New Generation Publishing offers a proofreading service to help make your work as close to perfect as possible. Again, if this is of interest to you, just ask!

Book Distribution

Do you buy books from Amazon and other retailers online like Waterstones, BOOKS *etc*. and Barnes & Noble?

All New Generation Publishing packages contain full distribution, meaning that your published book will appear on the pages of these household name retailers. In addition, your book will be available to order through high-street retailers, providing your potential audience with all the options they need to purchase your book.

Many authors will also want to target other countries and continents, and with New Generation Publishing we will make your book available not just in the UK but worldwide – whether its Barnes & Noble in the US, Kalahari.net in South Africa, Dymocks in Australia, Flipkart in India or Amazon EU in Europe.

Distribution is key when becoming a published author – without it your book will be unavailable to potential customers, thereby compromising sales. When launching a new product to the market, wholesale and distribution must be in place; without this your sales will be reduced.

New Generation Publishing offers an unrivalled distribution service to all its published authors.

Self-publishing with NGP ensures that your book is available to a global market.

Identifying a Genre

The first thing you need to do with your book is pick a genre. What's a genre? A themed bookshelf in a bookstore – or the top level(s) of book categories on a website. If your market is your audience, then your genre is your first narrowing of audience.

Don't be afraid of picking *one* genre. Trust us; it won't limit your sales, for two reasons:

1. If your book takes off, it won't matter what genre it started out in. Books can transcend genre; that is, they can sell to people who wouldn't normally buy them.
2. Specialised genre categories sell more books than general fiction. What's the least-respected of all genres? Romance (sad but true). What's the bestselling of all genres? Romance.

Putting your book in its correct genre helps it sell. After all, what sells better: a book on a shelf, or a book that never makes it to the shelf? If your book could go in one of a number of genres, work on finding out which genre has more readers who will buy your book – either by looking for similar books in the genre that are selling well, or by getting dedicated readers of that genre to read the book and tell you whether it's a winner or not.

Identifying a Subgenre

Do you need to identify a subgenre? Yes and no. At least, you need to identify whether your book is part of a subgenre or not. If it is, you will make more money if you work that into your marketing later on, when you can say your book is 'steampunk' rather than just science fiction, or urban fantasy rather than just fantasy – for example, when you're trying to get book reviewers to read your book.

Everyone has a favourite genre or two, and everyone has a couple of sweet spots within that genre. Identifying your subgenre means knowing about the current sweet spots in your book's genre.

How do you do that?
Read. A lot. And don't just read books, read the *news* related to your books. If you write steampunk, find out the sites where steampunk fans tend to rhapsodise about developments in the genre and in the world surrounding the genre. Sometimes a subculture evolves around a subgenre (or maybe it's the reverse). If you write zombies, read zombies.

Identifying a subgenre leads to all kinds of interesting marketing strategies.

Marketing Your Book

The reason that marketing is important is that nobody knows about you or your work when you first start out.

Without marketing, nobody will buy your book.

With marketing, people will know whether they want to look closer at your book. (Again, marketing is about identifying what your book *is* to your potential readers, not in hyping it up beyond all recognition just to get some attention.)

When you publish a book independently, at first you should have a brief surge of sales, from your family, friends, and other direct contacts. Then, as you run out of people you know willing to buy copies, those sales will drop off.

You need to find a way to get people who don't know you to find out about your book, and while having your family and friends brag about you is helpful, there are faster ways to accomplish it.

'New Generation Publishing are interested in selling books and ebooks' – sounds quite obvious coming from a publisher, doesn't it?

Well not really. Most self-publishing companies are not interested in selling your book – all they are interested in is selling you more marketing services, and to do so giving you the hope that more books will sell. At New Generation Publishing we put free advice first to identify what will best suit your needs.

The introduction of new marketing services has given our authors a wider choice of products that has helped get their books noticed and sold – as a result, our latest royalty statements have been the strongest on record.

This success of our authors' book sales has also been as a result of their use of our free marketing support system. As we always say to our authors, 'the cost of advice is free.'

Free Marketing Support

New Generation Publishing are the only self-publishing company to offer a free marketing support service to all authors no matter their budget.

Once your book has been published and 'gone live' we offer you the opportunity to book an appointment with us either by phone or face to face.

We will then spend between 30 minutes to an hour explaining all the marketing options available to you at no extra cost.

The conversation comes from years of experience and knowledge of the success of other authors – what they have achieved and how they went about it.

We will also explain what not to do!

Our most successful authors following a strategic plan that we help you put together, they will then update us and book in more consultations as required.

We have clearly seen in every royalty period, that the authors we speak to the most are usually the most successful.

This service is completely free for all our published authors, the question is: why?

Well quite simply if we help you sell more books, we are all winners!

What will it cost?

New Generation Publishing offers a range of self-publishing packages designed to meet all authors' needs, requirements and budgets. We offer the Standard Package, Advanced Package, Premier Package, Bookseller Package and Bestseller Package. Each publishing package contains four common elements: publication, typographical layout, global distribution and personal support.

In order to guarantee satisfaction for the author, we will send electronic proofs enabling them to see how the book will look once published. If at this stage, the author wishes to make changes, they can and the first set of changes will be made completely free of charge.

Until we receive written confirmation from the author that they are completely satisfied by the typographical layout and the cover design, we will not proceed with the publication.

When an author publishes a book with New Generation Publishing, we want to ensure that the author has as much control as possible over all elements of the book publication process. We also understand that each author has different levels of understanding when it comes to publishing a book. This is why we have experienced staff on hand to answer any questions you have throughout the entire process.

Overleaf are summaries of each of our five publishing packages.

Standard Package

£399.00

The New Generation Publishing Standard Package offers everything the author on a budget needs to become a fully published author and have their title available worldwide for potential customers to buy.

The Standard Publishing Package comprises of:

- ✓ Conversion of Word file, supplied by author into PDF with typographical layout to ensure a top quality book appearance.
- ✓ Cover design taken from chosen template or from own cover supplied, guidelines available.
- ✓ ISBN registration.
- ✓ Full distribution, ensuring your book is available via all major online outlets such as Amazon and Kobo and for high-street bookshops, such as Waterstones, to order.

Advanced Package

£699.00

The New Generation Publishing Advanced Package offers everything the Standard Package contains as well as some marketing, promotion, bespoke cover design and a hardback edition.

The package offers a cost-effective way to become a fully published author, with worldwide availability and a start to your marketing and promotion campaign.

The Advanced Publishing Package comprises of:

- ✓ Conversion of Word file, supplied by author into PDF with typographical layout to ensure a top-quality book appearance.
- ✓ ISBN registration.
- ✓ Full distribution, ensuring your book is available via all major online outlets such as Amazon and Kobo and for high-street bookshops, such as Waterstones, to order.
- ✓ Hardback edition additionally created with full distribution
- ✓ Bespoke cover design.
- ✓ Tailored press release created for the author.

Premier Package

£999.00

The New Generation Publishing Premier Package offers everything the Advanced Package contains, as well as increasing the level of marketing and promotion. The additional Press Release, Marketing Questionnaire and Marketing Kit will give you a great platform to start your marketing and promotion campaign.

The Premier Publishing Package comprises of:

- ✓ Conversion of Word file, supplied by author into PDF with typographical layout to ensure a top-quality book appearance.
- ✓ ISBN registration.
- ✓ Full distribution, ensuring your book is available via all major online outlets such as Amazon and Kobo and for high-street bookshops, such as Waterstones, to order.
- ✓ Hardback edition additionally created with full distribution
- ✓ Bespoke cover design.
- ✓ Press Release Package containing a professionally written press release tailored to you and your book and then distributed to over 500 media contacts.
- ✓ Marketing Questionnaire provided to support the author's promotional work.
- ✓ Marketing Kit (100 bookmarks, 100 postcards and 100 business cards) containing direct marketing materials featuring the author's cover, title, ISBN and retail price.

Bookseller Publishing Package

£1,799.00

The New Generation Publishing Bookseller Package offers everything the Premier Package contains as well as combining our premium marketing and promotional services.

Our unique Bookseller Service means that your book will actually be in the hands of an experienced independent bookseller – a first in the self-publishing industry.

The Bookseller Publishing Package comprises of:

- ✓ Conversion of Word file, supplied by author into PDF with typographical layout to ensure a top-quality book appearance.
- ✓ ISBN registration.
- ✓ Full distribution, ensuring your book is available via all major online outlets such as Amazon and Kobo and for high-street bookshops, such as Waterstones, to order.
- ✓ Hardback edition additionally created with full distribution
- ✓ Bespoke cover design
- ✓ Press Release Package containing a professionally written press release tailored to you and your book and then distributed to over 500 media contacts.
- ✓ Marketing Questionnaire provided to support the author's promotional work
- ✓ Marketing Kit (100 bookmarks, 100 postcards and 100 business cards) containing direct marketing materials featuring the author's cover, title, ISBN and retail price.
- ✓ Advertising in the *Writers Forum* magazine – your book will appear along side seven other titles in a full colour advert showing your book cover, description, ISBN and retail price.

- ✓ Featured Book – your book will feature alongside five others on the front page of our website as one of our 'Books of the Month', a press release will also be sent to media contacts informing them of our six 'Books of the Month'
- ✓ Bookseller Service – your book will feature for one month with an independent bookseller who will market and promote your book to bookshops throughout the UK.

Bestseller Package

£2,999.00

New Generation is proud to present the Bestseller Publishing Package, which offers authors the chance to give their book the best possible treatment while still offering great value for money.

The Bestseller Publishing Package comprises of:

- ✓ Conversion of Word file, supplied by author into PDF with typographical layout to ensure a top-quality book appearance.
- ✓ ISBN registration.
- ✓ Full distribution, ensuring your book is available via all major online outlets such as Amazon and Kobo and for high-street bookshops, such as Waterstones, to order.
- ✓ Hardback edition additionally created with full distribution
- ✓ Bespoke cover design
- ✓ Press Release Package containing a professionally written press release tailored to you and your book and then distributed to 500 media contacts
- ✓ Marketing Questionnaire provided to support the author's promotional work
- ✓ Marketing Kit (100 bookmarks, 100 postcards and 100 business cards) containing direct marketing materials featuring the author's cover, title, ISBN and retail price.
- ✓ Advertising in the *Writers Forum* magazine – your book will appear along side seven other titles in a full colour advert showing your book cover, description, ISBN and retail price.
- ✓ Featured Book – your book will feature alongside five others on the front page of our website as one of our 'Books of the Month', a press release will also be sent to media contacts informing them of our six 'Books of the Month'

- ✓ Bookseller Service – your book will feature for one month with an independent bookseller who will market and promote your book to bookshops throughout the UK.
- ✓ BOOKS *etc* Service – your book will be advertised on the front page of the BOOKS *etc* website and have its details sent to their database of over 1 million book buyers.
- ✓ Proofreading – a literary professional will correct any spelling, punctuation, grammar and other typographical errors in your manuscript.
- ✓ Media Service – our media officer will contact five local radio stations and local newspapers to try and arrange interviews / reviews / coverage. Media training will also be provided if required to ensure you get the best from your promotional opportunities
- ✓ Ebook Conversion – we will convert your manuscript to the ebook format and not just make it available on Kindle but also Kobo, Nook, iBooks, Sony e-reader etc.

Ebook Publishing

from £90

Would you like to sell your ebook on Kindle, iPad, NOOK, Kobo and other devices?

We are constantly looking to offer ground-breaking services at New Generation Publishing for our authors, to ensure we place them and their work right at the forefront of the market.

As a result, we are delighted to offer our authors the chance to also have their work available as an ebook. Not only this, but we will have their work converted to compatible files, ensuring their ebooks can be viewed with the major devices, such as the Kindle or the iPad. Furthermore, the ebooks will be distributed via the world's leading digital content distributors and available at e-retail stores worldwide.

Breaking news: NGP also now has direct agreements with Gardners, Overdrive and Amazon for distribution of its ebooks

Finally, writers will receive 55% royalty of sales revenue received by NGP and, with no print costs, this ensures an excellent revenue stream for the writers, as well as potential great success for their work.

The Print-On-Demand Process

Files for printing
The file formats we normally work with for the inside pages are:

- Print-quality PDF files
- Microsoft Word files

Our preference is a basic Word file, which will let us typeset the manuscript for you.

Binding styles
We provide a full range of binding styles:

- Perfect binding: also called paperback or square back binding.
- Thread sewing: the book is bound by machine-sewing folded sections together.
- Stitch sewn: the book is bound by gluing together folded sections that have been stitched with wire.
- Loose-leaf binding: individual pages are shrink-wrapped, drilled and presented in a ring binder, ideal for reference and training materials. We can organise the production of ring binders.
- Wire-o binding: useful for reference books, cookery books, manuals and material for photocopying as the pages lay flat.
- Wire stitching: also called saddle stitching, this is used on journals, magazines, booklets and other short publications.

Note on binding: different types will only be available with certain book sizes, and higher prices will apply for more complex binding types. For a paperback, perfect binding is used as standard unless otherwise requested.

Maintaining availability
Authors' books will automatically be available globally via print-on-demand for a full 12 months. The author will then be offered the opportunity to renew the books' availability for a small fee (£25+Vat) at the end of each 12-month period.

Author orders
Authors can also order copies of their own work at a discounted cost. The amount of discount depends on the size of order – the greater the quantity, the greater the discount we will receive from the printer. Authors can provide New Generation Publishing with a range of quantities and we will be happy to quote for each. Our quotations will include packaging and delivery to you.

Why New Generation Publishing?

New Generation Publishing understands the needs and requirements of authors.

Our team has senior experience in both traditional publishing and self-publishing and we know what is required for authors when they are looking to publish a book.

Our publishing packages and marketing services have been designed in order to accommodate authors across all budgets and experience in book publishing, marketing and promotion.

We have identified some key requirements for authors:

Personal approach
We like to talk to our authors before, during and after the publishing of their book – we feel it is in all of our interests to create a relationship so that both author and publisher clearly understand the expectations of both parties. We also want that communication to continue after the book has been published – we are interested in helping, listening and hearing news, and the help and advice is free.

Retail pricing
When you publish a book with New Generation Publishing your book will be priced competitively. Too many self-publishing companies price their authors' books at such a high price that it makes it very difficult to sell and market. We also understand that certain books do require a higher price based on the nature of the subject or genre, where applicable.

Distribution
Distribution and availability is key for any product and we make all our published books available to a global audience. Your book will be available with online retailers worldwide and listed on the systems

of most high-street retailers. This enables your book to be available globally, thereby increasing the sales opportunities.

Marketing

New Generation Publishing is continuously looking to develop new and unique services for authors. We have our unique Bookseller Service, placing books with an independent bookseller who works with bookstores to sell copies of your book. We have partnerships with major retailers, such as BOOKS *etc.* which allows our published books to be placed on their homepage and marketed to their database of over one million book buyers. We can also offer our authors a critique service, media services, through to more regular marketing services unique to New Generation Publishing.

Experience

The combined management experience of New Generation Publishing in both traditional publishing and self-publishing means that all authors' needs, requirements and expectations can be highlighted at the outset and met. If in any case this cannot happen then the partnership will never begin and we will advise the author that they are not the best fit for New Generation Publishing.

Remember...

You have complete control over every aspect of the publishing and production of *your* book(s). We will give you advice and make suggestions, but the final decision on format, page and cover design, paper, cover material and finish and binding style rests with you.

You can also print as many as you would like. However, it is a false economy to print more than you are likely to sell. We will advise you and provide quotations for different print quantities.

If you are looking for something bespoke, just provide us with an outline of your ideas or proposal and we will provide an initial quotation. We will constantly revise our quotation as details become clearer. Remember our advice is free and we do not ask for any payment in advance of the package.

Can you visit us?
You certainly can. Our head office is based on Fleet Street in London and we also have an office in Buckinghamshire. Simply make an appointment by calling 01234 711956 or by email to:
info@newgeneration-publishing.com

What our Authors say

The following is just a small excerpt from out testimonial page from our website.

Delighted!
Dear Sam, Thank you for the e-mail, accepting my wish for a RRP. I have to say that I'm really overwhelmed by the outstanding service that you are giving me. How delighted I've been when you've accepted the modifications that I have discovered along the way. Thank you so much again. (quote me if you like).

Bob A

Absolutely delighted!
I was delighted when the very first copy of my latest book, 'Sam's Magic Surfboard' dropped through my letter box a couple of days ago. Although this is the third book that I have published with New Generation Publishing, I still got a big thrill when I opened the package and saw my latest book 'in the flesh'. It is rather like greeting a new born child for the first time. I am more than satisfied with the final result. NGP's production team led by Sam Rennie have done a brilliant job, and have been so helpful during the whole process. Nothing was too much trouble for Sam and his crew! I would have no hesitation in recommending NGP to any new authors who are not sure of how to get their work into print. A very good job from a friendly company who put their Authors first!

John Phipps

The Wedding's Season
Dear Sam, Today I received by mail my copy of the novel 'The Wedding's Season.' I am deeply touched by the quality of the published book. All elements I am finding high quality and a lot of attention given, and I am grateful for your effort. With best regards to all of you,

Artur Friedberg

Thanks!
I'm elated with my published work. I look forward to working on the third, but I just wanted to say a big thank you again to you and your team. Kind regards,

Tom Gaskin , author of Search of the Lost

My day's been brightened!
Hope this finds you well, having a sunny afternoon! You'll never guess - UPS just delivered my author copy of Blizzard Puddle and the Postal Phoenix. The book is more astounding than I envisaged and, as with each past publication, am utterly bowled over! Please pass along my wholehearted thanks to all team members who worked exceedingly hard on my children's novel. My day's been brightened beyond compare; thank you so very much. Best wishes

Matthew Boulton

Thank you!!
It was great to see you last evening. On behalf of everyone at the event, may I extend my warmest thanks to you for what proved to be a fascinating discussion, from which all of us, current and potential NGP clients alike, gained much benefit. After you left and we took a break, everyone was buzzing with excitement and chatting nineteen to the dozen. In fact, when I tried to resume the meeting, I had to call them to order and settle them down! It was a great success. Thank you.

Mike Richards

Absolutely awesome job done on the book
Firstly, what an absolutely awesome job done on the book. It really is looking great and I am so very pleased about the end product, thank you to you and your team. I am indeed very, very happy with the end product so once again thank you. Great news about the ebook work.

Simon

You must get fed up with me thanking you but I really do mean it
Hi Daniel/Sam, Just to let you know the three books have all arrived - really is all too exciting for an old man like me!!!!!!!!!!! Anyway, you must get fed up with me thanking you but I really do mean it. Also, I am now beginning to push the new website out in to the market place

so it will be interesting to see if any extra sales come from it. Hope you both have a good weekend, Thanks again, Very best regards,

Andy C

The personal relationship with authors is definitely a plus
Once again we'd like to say how pleased we have been with the whole process and how helpful both David and Sam – and now you – have been. The personal relationship with authors is definitely a plus and we will certainly recommend New Generation Publishing to all our contacts.

Janet and Paul Clark

We could not have asked for a better service
We would however like to thank New Generation for the excellent customer service and help with the publication of our book. We could not have asked for a better service. Good luck in the future

Dave and Jane Whitfield

Plan to stay with you guys for as long as possible
In 2 weeks from now, it will have been a year since we published 'Greener on The Other Side'. It has been a very exciting and enlightening ride. I am very thankful for your services for that. All in all, I am very pleased with NPG and plan to stay with you guys for as long as possible. What I really liked this past year from NPG was the communication I had with Sam. I appreciated the speed at which you sent books when I requested them. I also appreciated you sending copies to the Caine Prize for African Literature (even though we have a long way to go).

Lionel Ntasano

This is to express my sincere thanks and appreciation to New Generation Publishing
This is to express my sincere thanks and appreciation to New Generation Publishing for producing a well designed and beautiful book. Frankly speaking, when I opened the parcel and saw the book, I thought my eyes were playing tricks on me. You have made me one among the happiest people this x-mas season. I didn't know that your company could do so well. Let me make a confession. Since 2010,

while I was writing and searching for a would-be publisher, I noticed in my box emails from your company up to 2014. When ever I see New Generation Publishing among my mails, I'll delete it. I was only communicating with Dorrance Publishing Company, Raider Publishing Company, PublishAmerica and many others. Notwithstanding, I was not satisfy with there fees, contract and the time it takes to have the book publish. One day I decided to respond to New Generation Publishing by writing a letter of enquiry. The reply I received including the materials sent were very much encouraging. It was at this point I decided to do business with you. I must admit, your publications are GREAT. May God continue to bless all the reagents of your company. I WISH YOU ALL MERRY X-MAS AND A HAPPY AND PROSPEROUS NEW YEAR.

Daniel Dalton

After a few phone calls I opted for New Generation Publishing
Self publication - previously termed "vanity publishing" - was now an acceptable option. Research commenced. The internet led me to many companies offering services from an expensive bespoke package to printing. After a few phone calls I opted for New Generation Publishing who offered a deal which suited me at an affordable cost. The book would be produced and marketed on Amazon, Waterstones online and the publisher's website. They would sort out the IBSN number. All I had to do was email the manuscript from my laptop and choose some photographs from a selection provided from which my book cover was designed. I sat on Rhossili Bay to write the blurb needed for the back cover. I would receive royalties from each book sold and could buy the book direct at a reduced price to sell myself. A hardback version of the book arrived and I experienced the same rush of adrenalin as the main character in my book has when he rides a winner. I held it, a tangible item. I was ready to move on to the next stage - marketing and selling.

Daniela Mylot

A huge thank you for all your efforts
Firstly, may I just say, and I believe I speak on behalf of every author who initially published through Authors Online, a huge thank you for all your efforts and for allowing our publications to continue being

available, it really is very much appreciated. I can only imagine how much time & work was involved, so thanks to you all at New Generation Publishing. I can confirm that there is no issue with the availability of my particular book, as an associate was able to purchase a copy through Amazon only a week or so ago, and it was delivered in good time.

Chris (Panikos Christodoulou)

Superb efficient first-class service
Sam has the patience of a Saint, my e-mails were responded to almost immediately and I was always kept up to date with the process. In short I wouldn't dream of going anywhere else to have my books published and would fully recommend it to all aspiring writers.

James Evans - Time Cure

For any aspiring writers out there
For any aspiring writers out there, I cannot think of a better place to start your quest. The realms of publishing are indeed a daunting place, but the diligent and knowledgeable team at NGP will be your ultimate guide. I may only be a fledgling author myself, but the service provided thus far has given me the information, resources (and self-belief) I need to take my work to the next level. Long story short? Talk to New Generation Publishing today and realise your dream!

Adam J. Watts

Contact us today!

Head Office:
New Generation Publishing, 107-111 Fleet Street,
London EC4A 2AB

Buckinghamshire Office:
New Generation Publishing, Olney House, 17 High Street, Olney,
Buckinghamshire, MK46 4EB

01234 711 956
0207 936 9941
info@newgeneration-publishing.com

New Generation Publishing
www.newgeneration-publishing.com
@NGPublishing

New Generation Publishing

www.ingramcontent.com/pod-product-compliance
Lightning Source LLC
LaVergne TN
LVHW041311080426

835510LV00009B/956